Hello, I am a mature student at Gloucester College taking a GCSE in English.

Having left school in the sixties with no qualifications I went to work in the engineering industry. I have lived in Gloucester since the seventies when I met my wife and got married. I have three grown-up children and two grandchildren. You will hear of Harry and Freya later on in the book in the poem *My Grandson Harry*.

John Wood Philips

IS IT ME, OR IS IT MY AGE?

AUSTIN MACAULEY PUBLISHERS™

LONDON • CAMBRIDGE • NEW YORK • SHARJAH

A CIP catalogue record for this title is available from the British Library.

ISBN 9781787101326 (Paperback)
ISBN 9781787101333 (E-Book)

www.austinmacauley.com

First Published (2018)
Austin Macauley Publishers Ltd.
25 Canada Square
Canary Wharf
London
E14 5LQ

Acknowledgements

Many thanks to all of those people who encouraged me to keep on writing these poems and to get them published into a book.

A special mention to John Mvula, my friend who helped me collate all my poems and prepare this book for publication.

Gloucester College who helped me with the course I was taking and without whom I would never have started writing poetry.

All my friends at the Brunswick Baptist church, Gloucester City Mission and Gloucester Salvation Army for all their free food and drinks they have supplied me with over the past two years.

Without their encouragement I would have given up all hope a long time ago.

**To you all a big
THANK YOU.**

Foreword

It all started for me in September of 2013 when I decided to start taking an evening course in photography. Little was I to know what would happen then. There I was, well into my course taking photographs of my given subject of the week. We were told to keep a portfolio of our work so that it could be displayed at the end of the term. This I did and started showing friends some of the photos I had taken. They were very good, but rather boring to look at, so, I decided to start writing poems to go along with some of my photos to describe why I took that particular picture. The first few I wrote were about nature: a spider, a bee, autumn leaves and then the tall ship in the docks undergoing renovation. After showing these to my friends I started getting comments on how good they were, and then suddenly out of the blue I was getting words coming into my head, often at two or three in the morning. I would wake and find that I was unable to sleep, so many words were drifting around inside my head I just had to write them down.

As soon as my pen touched the paper off I would go, words would pour into my head from where I knew not. I found I was writing these verses of poetry that I simply had no idea I could write. All of these poems were written by me at a time when I was going through different emotions, as you will be able to tell from the poems themselves. Some are poignant, some are true. Some are based on true facts, others are entirely fictional; I will leave you to decide which are which. Either way, I hope you all enjoy them as much as I enjoyed writing them.

CONTENTS

Gloucester Life

Famous People

World Events

That's Life

WHO WILL CARE?

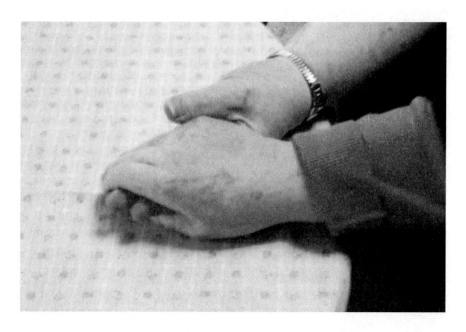

A selection of poems all about the state of care or the lack of it in this country. Some of these poems are based on true facts, others are entirely fictional. I will leave you to decide which is which.

Who Cares?

My friend has just come out of hospital,
They've found him a place in a home.
I went there to see him a while ago,
And found him, in his room, all alone.
He went to the lounge a few times,
But he was the only man in the room.
Sat there between five old ladies,
His only companion was gloom.

He ate in the dining room, the first days,
But half of them could have been dead.
The staff had to come around and wake them,
In order that they could be fed.
With four operations on his stomach,
They say he is really quite ill.
And the money he got from his house sale,
They're using to pay his care bill.

So now he stays in his bedroom,
For ten to twelve hours on his own,
Just waiting for someone to visit,
Or maybe, a call on his phone.
I promised to see him again soon,
Just like his friends from the club.
Who never have once gone to see him,
It seems their friend, they now snub.

My friend was quite downcast and saddened
He used to be cheerful and bright.
So I went back to see him this morning,
And found that he'd died in the night.

Forgotten Hero

A man stops to think,
As he cuddles his drink,
Like a mother protecting her baby.
Will he eat today?
It's too early to say,
I doubt it, but then again, maybe.
He fought in the war,
God knows what he saw,
His mates were all killed by a shell.
Now he reminisces,
Of the friends that he misses,
The stories this poor man could tell.
People rushing by,
The man starts to cry.
No Christmas with family for him.
How alone he must feel,
His only Christmas meal,
Is the one he might find in a bin.
Christmas morning,
Without any warning,
The man hears a voice in his head.
"You've outlived your life,
Now come join your wife",
Then the man realises he's dead.
Next time you're in town,
Take a good look around,
You will be surprised what you see.
That vagabond, tramp,
In clothes cold and damp
Just imagine, that could be me.

The Life Line

The Gov had just cut my money; I've not enough to pay my rent.
When I get my pension tomorrow, I know that it's already spent.
My utilities I pay by the meter, I've cut everything to the core.
Now I've got a letter from the bailiffs, so I wait for the knock on the door.
I'm already surviving on hand outs, there isn't any food left at home.
Did I read somewhere in the Bible, "man cannot live off bread alone"?
I've lived on my own for some years now, without the need of a dog or a cat.
I've been ill, and I need looking after, but it seems I can forget about that.

Everyday seems to be getting harder, as I'm writing this poem I sigh.
Is life like this, really worth it? Or should I just curl up and die?
I've just been handed a life line, seems I have Age UK to thank.
They gave me a red slip of paper, now I'm off to my local food bank.
They gave me enough food for three days; at least today I can eat.
All things for a good balanced diet, Pasta, Fruit, Veg and Meat.
During the time I was waiting, they sat me down with a drink,
And a companion to talk to, and some time to calm down and think.

I was at the end of my tether, I had nowhere else left to go,
What would have happened tomorrow, well I simply don't know.
All my optioned had been exhausted, I was about to give up all hope,
I had contemplated with suicide, with the help of a long piece of rope.
They tell me I'm one of hundreds, of people they get through their door,
Each week their numbers are growing, does this government realise the
score?
We're living in the twenty first century, this shouldn't be happening today!
To all those who donate to food banks, THANK YOU is all I can say.

The Broken Man

Yesterday I saw a grown man, left broken and in tears,
Unable to pay the bills, and his mortgage arrears.
As he told me his story, I just started to sob,
He was leaving his family, after losing his job.
With no money coming in, he was left in no doubt,
That in no time at all, his funds would run out.
After leaving for work, at the start of each day!
He hoped, upon hope, something new comes his way.

After trying for months, he could no longer cope,
He was ending it all, with the help of a rope.
To his wife and children, a letter he'd wrote,
And he pulled from his pocket, this suicide note.
"I've something to tell you, I should let you know!
You see, I lost my job, a few months ago."
"I tried to tell you, but the time wasn't right,
As the whole world's against me, I give up the fight."

"Please tell the children, I'm sorry my dear!
There'll be no Holiday, or Christmas this year."
"Tell them, that I love them, and maybe when they've grown,
They'll understand that you're all, better off on your own."
At this point in time, I just had to confess,
I found myself, years ago, in a similar mess.
Pulled myself together, and went back to my wife,
By the end of the year, we had made a new life.

After talking, the man said, "that now he had seen,
Looking back at the past, what a fool he had been."
He would no longer try to bear life's burdens alone,
And went back to his wife, his children, and home.

Let's Hope

We took the kids to see their Gran,
They say it's been a while.
Since they saw her wrinkled face,
With such a lovely smile.

But when they got to see her,
She shouted "GO AWAY"
She didn't recognise them,
As she's not herself today.

The kids were really upset,
So we tried a second time.
She was loving, she was caring,
She was absolutely fine.

At times it's hard to see her,
Just sitting in her chair,
Oblivious to everything,
As if there's no one there.

My father he has given her,
Three quarters of his life,
Now he's living with a stranger,
Although she's still his wife

To see him broken hearted,
Left all of us in tears,
Unable to communicate,
With his wife of Forty years.
Now they've put her in a care home,
Cause my father couldn't cope,
With no more we can do for her!
There's nothing left but hope.

Such Style and Such Grace

She's gone now but never forgotten,
No one else could ever replace!
The woman I married all those years ago,
Who walked with such style and such grace!

Look at her now she's so beautiful,
So peacefully she lies in her bed!
To see her you'd think she was sleeping,
No reason to think she was dead.

No more body creased up in torture!
No more painful expression on her face!
But the woman I knew just a year ago,
Who walked with such style and such grace!

For twelve months she'd been bravely fighting,
That cancerous enemy within,
Attacking throughout her whole body,
From deep beneath her own skin.

Those sickening months of the Chemo,
The side effects from all of the drugs,
Then unable to fight off infection,
Brought by the tiniest of bugs.

I remember the day I first saw her,
The sweetest of smiles on her face!
The girl I first kissed in the schoolyard,
Who walked with such style and such grace!

Story of a Street Boy

Mama Leslie was tidying the boys' room, when the Pastor approached her in tears.
"There's a new boy come into the office, I've not seen such a bad case in years."
The young boy sat huddled in the office, between two people curled up in a ball,
She glanced at the young boy and noticed, he was dirty, quite frail and so small.
His social worker handed her a folder, she opened it and read the first page,
It said the boys' name was Carlos he was twelve but small for his age.
After reading only the first page, not believing the things she had saw,
In her throat she got a large lump, and found it hard to read any more.

She put the file down on the table, picked the boy up, sat him down on her knee,
It was like picking up a child's rag doll, he weighed barely more than a flee.
"You'll be safe here," said Mama Leslie, with tears welling up in her eyes,
As the Pastor lifted the boys T shirt, showing all the bruises to their surprise.
Everyone except Carlos was tearful, he had no more tears left to cry,
He'd obviously been treated so cruelly, now they all wanted to find out why,
"I had to look after the chickens, one died, then grabbing me by the jaw,
My uncle punched me in the stomach, then kicked me whilst I lay on the floor."

It was then that one of the neighbours, came over and he rescued me,
He put me inside of his vehicle, and brought me into the DSWD.
Paolo and Bong two other children, who had come to the office to see,
Their new arrival in person, then took him off to watch some T.V.
Carlos was raised in Manila, notorious for its drug abuse and vice,
He lived for a while with his Grandma, he'd already been homeless twice.
All of his family were drug addicts, his mother uncle Paco and his wife,
If it had not been for that neighbour, Carlos would have sure lost his life.

This poem is based on a true story. Carlos is now a grown man working for Helping Hands Healing Hearts Ministries, Helping other children.

My Last Summer

Throughout the days of my last summer,
I spent time with my friend.
I've Cancer and I'm dying,
But they've stayed with me till the end.

They visited me in hospital,
They spent time at my home!
Giving up the time they had,
So I wouldn't be alone.

During all the treatment, that
I've gone through these past years.
We've been together side by side,
Through the suffering and the tears.

We knew that I was dying,
Of that there was no doubt.
They helped me organize my death,
For when my time runs out.

Now today it is my funeral,
They stand there at my grave.
Until it's time to meet again,
Be brave, my friend, be brave.

The Holi day Home!

Our Auntie Olive's crazy,
Though we say so ourselves,
She sits there in her bedroom,
Amongst the Fairies and the Elves.

We can't have a conversation,
For she knows not what we say,
She sits there in her bedside chair,
And she gently starts to sway.

We took her to the Doctors,
But there's nothing they can do,
Month by month she's getting worse,
That much we know is true.

So we took her to a "Holiday Home"!
Where we had to leave her there,
Now she sits there in her bedroom,
Simply rocking in her chair.

NATURE

A selection of poems all about nature and the things
That were all around me and my home,
This is how it all started. Whilst I was taking these photographs I started
writing poems to go with them.

Autumn Leaves

Autumn leaves falling without any sound,
Floating like feathers they fall to the ground.
And cover the surface with colours so bold,
A beautiful carpet, of red, brown and gold.
Then the wind comes along and during the day,
The leaves one by one drift slowly away.

The Humble Bee

He flies around for hours and hours,
Visiting all sorts of flowers.
Every single plant and tree,
Relies upon the Humble Bee.
Supplying him with nectar sweat,
To make honey for us to eat.
Dusting his head with pollen bright,
To take away with him in flight.
Cross pollination is what we need,
So that on their fruit we all can feed.
I hope with this you'll all agree,
And help to save the Humble Bee.

(Gloucester is now the world's first Bee Guardian City.)

It's Spring?

The Crocuses and Daffodils,
Have all started to appear.
Maybe they're the beginning signs,
That finally, spring is here.

Though the weather, we have had,
Of late, has left us all in doubt.
With even more rain, forecast our way,
And then, today the sun is out.

Each morning when I wake up,
All the birds begin to sing.
The sun is up by six o clock,
Such joy these things all bring.

Looking all around me,
At the water covered ground.
More evidence that spring IS here,
In small places I have found.

It's been a farmers' nightmare,
With some crops still to be sown.
And fields to wet to take machines,
Their hopes will soon be blown.

Any crops the farmers try to sow,
The fields just turn to mud.
But the signs ARE here, just look around,
As the trees come into bud.

Joys of Spring

With the blossom all around me growing,
And the tops of the trees to and froing.
In the warm gentle breeze,
All my woes seem to ease,
And the smile on my face is soon showing.

With the birds in the morning all singing,
To the branches and wires tightly clinging,
In a chorus of song,
You can hear all day long,
A much brighter day they're all bringing.

With the sun in the sky gently shining,
All my worries are slowly declining.
In its warm gentle ray,
As the children all play,
My chores for today I'm refining.

With the flowers in the garden all blooming,
Spring is here now, I'm assuming.
All their colours so bright,
Keep reflecting the light,
As lawns, shrubs and hedges I'm grooming.

With the lambs in the fields gaily leaping,
And the ewes close by gently sleeping.
In the warmth of the sun,
They gamble and run,
But their mothers a close watch are keeping.

The Lambs

I stood there for a moment,
And watched them for a while,
The little lambs were gambling,
Slowly my face began to smile.

So many ewes were out there,
Lambing season had begun,
I realise looking around me,
I'm sure that spring has sprung.

The lambs would start off running,
Then jump off all four feet,
Then realise that Mum had gone,
And they'd give a little bleat.

But Mum was close by watching,
She'd give a gentle bah,
Then little ones came running,
They hadn't gone that far!

The milk bar was still open,
So they'd suckle from their mum,
Then after a few moments rest,
Off again they'd run.

To see the lambs out playing,
Just brought me so much joy,
And took me back some fifty years,
To times when I was a boy.

Just a Country Boy

Being just a country boy,
I lived a simple life,
The three things that I wished for,
A job, a home a wife.

Now when I was eleven,
I was sent to Newent School,
And placed into the D stream,
Where I was thought of as a fool.

I liked my art and history,
I was no good though at sport.
But I knuckled down in classes,
And I learned what I was taught.

I was told "respect your elders",
And to always be polite,
To recognise the differences,
Between what's wrong and right.

I got a job in engineering,
They said I was quite bright,
Gave half my wages to my mum,
Cause the money at home was tight.

In my sixty years of living,
I've learned a thing or two,
But every day I'm still learning,
Things, of which I had no clue.

Too Much Rain

For months it's been raining,
Through the day and night.
The future looks bleak,
As there's no end in sight.

Reservoirs are overflowing,
Into our rivers and streams,
Causing even more flooding,
To us all, or so it seems.

At Dawlish in Devon,
The rain and the gales, has
swept all the ballast,
From under the rails.

They say all this water,
And not enough trees,
Caused houses on cliff tops,
To fall into the seas.

The people in Somerset, Are
now, fed up to the hilt,
Seems the rivers and drains,
Are all clogged up with silt.

The men from the environment,
Say "there's just too much rain",
So they'll wait until next year,
When it all happens again.

Water, Water, Everywhere.

Water, water, everywhere,
And not a drop to drink.
Where the hell's it coming from?
It makes me stop to think.

Looking out my windows,
All around me is a lake.
Will this weather ever end?
I hope for peoples' sake.

Flooded out another year,
Losing everything they own.
No longer insured for loss of things,
Because their Insurance Premiums grown.

For weeks and weeks the wind has blown,
And the rain poured from the sky.
The whole countries waterlogged,
Now they know the reason why.

That thing they call the jet stream,
Keeps escaping from its tether.
And every time it runs amok
It brings us nasty weather.

Let's hope the good lord captures it,
And chains it to the mast.
Then all the water disappears,
And the sun comes out at last.

Red Sky

As I was walking home last night,
The redness of the sky.
Appeared over the horizon,
Into the corner of my eye.

I stopped and paused a moment,
And I wondered at the sight.
As the sun slowly disappeared,
And the day turned into night.

A good day we'll have tomorrow,
Folklore would have us think.
The light is gradually fading,
As the sun begins to sink.

A flock of birds fly over,
Formed in the usual v,
As all the birds go home to roost,
A wondrous sight to see.

As it's slowly getting darker,
The red clouds turn to grey.
The once blue sky, turns into black,
And now it's no longer day.

When I awake tomorrow,
I hope the folklore's right,
And as the sun arises,
The day is nice and bright.

Pretty In Pink

Here she stands in the churchyard,
Looking so pretty in pink.
Like a bridesmaid at a wedding,
So beautiful don't you think.

She stands with her arms wide open,
As if in praise to the sun.
Just inside the church entrance,
On full show to everyone.

The moment that I first saw her,
A photograph I soon took.
Then reached for my pen and paper,
And wrote this poem down in my book.

The Spider

Here she sits upon her web,
Of finely spun gossamer thread.
With deadly fangs and venom strong,
She'll sit there waiting all day long.
Then, suddenly she'll run and pounce,
On prey that weighs barely an ounce.
Then wrap them in cocoon so tight,
Then feast on them throughout the night.
She sucks out every drop of juice,
Then leaves her web, it has no use.

The Squirrel

With those bright eyes,
And large bushy tail.
He leaps tree to tree,
Without any fail.
Then scurries cross carpet,
Of leaves on the floor!
Searching for the larder,
He'd prepared months before.

Sitting bolt upright,
On only two feet.
He breaks into nut,
And savours the treat.
Whilst all of the time,
His ears scan the air!
For the sound of anything,
That's moving out there.

Hastily feeding on,
Nuts and Pine Cone!
Constantly fearful of,
Attack whilst alone,
Startled, he runs,
And climbs nearest tree!
Till safe, in the cover,
Of the large Canopy.

ME MYSELF AND I

All about me and the things that have happened to me.
Some of the things I love, and some that I see every day.
Not everything you read is true but based on things that are true.

The Birthday Cake

I'm sixty today, can't believe that it's true,
From birth until now the times simply flew.
I married, had kids bought a house of our own,
Worked most of my life whilst my kids have all grown.
Now I'm ill and not working, I'm just scraping by,
With nothing to live for, just waiting to die.
On Wednesdays to Fridays I go to the Brun,
Eat, drink and talk and sometimes have fun.
Now with my friends I can look to the light,
Their giving me guidance to do what is right.
With friends all around me, the right road I'll take,
And to help me along they have made me this cake.

(Then helped me to eat it)
Thanks to Evelyn who baked it.
The Brun is the Brunswick Baptist Church who run an open door.

The Stream Of Thoughts

At night when I lie in my bed,
These words appear inside my head.
Without thinking I just seem to find,
These words that come into my mind.
Like water seeping from a stone,
They just appear whilst I'm alone.

Like a river oozing from a spring,
Come words about the slightest thing.
They pick up pace, and very soon,
Become a torrent in the first Monsoon.
The river soon becomes a sea,
And I drown, in words of ecstasy.

The Lord Sayeth Unto Me

The lord spoke to me whilst in my bed,
And this is what the good lord said.
"Pick up your pen and follow me,
And soon another life you'll see.
Put away your thoughts of doubt,
For I will surely cast them out"

"Don't fight me, for you have no choice,
These words you hear are from MY voice.
I'll send them down like drops of rain,
That slowly soak into your brain.
For you to write with pen so swift,
And share with joy, this brand new gift."

When I Was a Youngster

When I was a youngster,
Fresh out of school.
Drainpipe trousers, frilly shirt,
I thought I was cool.

Listening to Caroline,
Broadcast from a ship,
Parked up in a lay-by,
We thought it was hip.

We only had three channels,
On black and white TVs.
We'd never heard of videos,
Let alone DVDs

The only entertainment,
We had in my day,
Was a transistor radio,
And records to play.

Now I'm not regretful,
Feeling sad or forlorn.
But young kids nowadays,
Don't know they've been born.

Those Long Halcyon Summer Days

Yesterday I thought of my school friends,
And all of the things that we did.
In those long halcyon days of the summer,
And the time that I spent as a kid.
We would all disappear for hours,
Playing games, running loose in the wood.
We had no worries of danger
Back then it was easy, we could.

We would all help out in the harvest,
Spending long days on the farm.
In those days there was no health and safety,
But we never came to much harm.
I would earn pocket money picking currents,
I saved up to buy my first bike.
One with a twelve speed derailleur,
Now I could go where I like.

We all played football or cricket,
For our local village team.
So many decades have passed now,
My childhood is all but a dream.
Years ago it seems we lost contact,
Reunions a few times I've tried.
Some have simply just moved on,
And sadly a couple have died.

Yesterday as I thought of my school days,
Reminiscing of the things that I did.
In those long halcyon days of the summer,
Oh the joys of just being a kid.

A Train of Thoughts

As I was a boy in the country, I'd often lie there and dream!
Of being the driver of an engine, Powered along by some steam.
With smoke coming out of the funnel Watching, I could but only admire,
The driver, standing there, with the stoker as he shovelled more coal into the
fire.

Our speed had gathered quite quickly, Soon into a tunnel we'd shoot!
The driver gave a tug of the lever and the whistle gave a loud TOOOOOT.
The weather was warm and still sunny, the wind in my hair, feeling great.
As he waved to all of the people, Trackside, from off the footplate.

As I looked out of the window, at the countryside passing by.
It brought back so many memories, along with a tear to my eye.
We were coming soon into the station, as we slowed down for the final bend.
The platform was gradually approaching, where our journey would come to
an end.

Today we had made it in good time, although at no time was it ever a race.
As I watched the passengers disembarking, Most had a big smile on their
face.
Some had taken a few photographs others had taken high tea!
But up front, stood there on the footplate, that's the place where I want to be.

Elderly Scholar

Here I am sixty,
An elderly man,
With no goal to aim for,
No business plan.

Since going to college,
A new focus I've found,
Taking photos, writing poetry,
I'm breaking new ground.

With people around me,
I've made a new start,
And found it quite easy,
Writing prose from the heart.

Most people tell me,
I'm doing quite well.
But I'm really not sure yet,
It's too soon to tell.

How Will I Know?

How do I know that he sees me?
How do I know that he's there?
How do I know that he hears me?
Whenever I'm saying a prayer;

They tell me he sees everybody!
He's with me where ever I go.
But he's with me only in spirit;
So tell me, how will I know?

Will he tap me on the shoulder?
Or whisper some words in my ear?
At night while I'm in my bed sleeping,
Will he then miraculously reappear?

Who will answer my questions?
How will I know that it's true?
Only I can give me the answer!
God loves me, and I know it, DO YOU?

I'm Tired of Being Ill

For over a year I've been tired,
The government is now tired of me,
So last week they sent me for a medical,
At ATOS down at my local DWP.

Each morning I wake up is different,
Some days full of vigour and vim,
Others, after eight hours of sleeping,
My bed all day long I stay in.

Over time I've seen lots of doctors,
I've had cameras pushed up either end.
Two years ago having bowel surgery,
I'm worried I cannot pretend.

I've been under eminent physicians,
Whose knowledge is out of my league?
With the results keep coming back negative,
They say I've got Chronic Fatigue.

I spoke to a specialist doctor,
Who said he thought it could be,
Having a viral infection,
Then a jab against Hepatitis C.

I had one when I went to Morocco,
A month later I felt really rough,
I've been ill on and off for ten years now,
And I'm thinking enough is enough.

Next month at Cheltenham General,
A camera capsule I have to take,
I'm hoping that they find a problem,
Just to prove to them that I'm no fake.

Aches and Pains of Old Age

Each morning when I wake up,
I try to put aside my pain,
And carry on regardless,
And a normal life maintain.

With the stiffness in my fingers,
My arms, my knees, my feet,
It's hard to do the simplest things,
And try not to face defeat.

When I try to put my socks on,
Or tie the laces in my shoe,
With Arthritis in so many joints,
These things are hard to do.

The Doctor says it's my old age,
There's nothing he can do.
So I guess I'll face the facts of life,
And try to muddle through.

I'm trying to keep active,
And not make too much fuss,
I walk the two miles into town,
As I've no pass for the bus.

My toe and foot are aching,
I hobble into the town,
It's taken half an hour so,
I need a quick sit down.

But after a long coffee,
And a catch up of the news,
My aches and pains I leave behind,
And forget about my blues.

Infectious Behaviour

Here I am, lying in my bed,
With runny nose and aching head!
Throat that's sore and dry as dust,
In medicines I'll have to trust.

So in my bed I'll have to stay,
With drink to last me through the day!
Hot water bottle at my feet,
That's generating lots of heat.

With aching bones, and feeling cold,
It's harder, now I'm getting old!
To fight off any small infection,
I'm glad I had that flu injection.

For three days now, I have been trying,
To get better, but I think I'm dying.
What's a bloke like me to do?
This ain't no cold, this is MAN FLU.

Patiently Waiting

I'm waiting at the doctors,
I need to be assessed,
On whether I can wash myself,
And manage to get dressed.

But my ability it changes,
Day by day, on how I feel,
To assess someone on just one day,
To myself seems so unreal.

Some days I awake, I'm full of beans,
I'm raring to get out.
Other days, I could just stay in bed,
Of that I have no doubt.

To keep fit and healthy,
I do my best each day,
I'm a minefield of activity,
But with a three hour time delay.

I do a little walking,
Some poetry I'll write,
But find it hard to stay awake,
As I'm restless in the night.

I'll do a little cooking,
Some cleaning if I can,
But find it hard to cope alone,
Cause, after all, I am a man.

My Grandson Harry

My grandson Harry has just turned three,
I really love him, I think he loves me!
He's just out of nappies, his parents are pleased,
He's using the toilet for poo poos and wees

He meets me for breakfast on most Saturdays,
Where he feeds the animals, runs around and plays.
He's up at six thirty most days as a rule,
And three times a week he goes to playschool.

He loves both his Grandmas, Aunt Lizzy and Mark,
Where sometimes he stays, goes walks in the park
Then there's Aunt Emma and his Uncle James,
And their daughter Freya with whom he plays games.

He loves his Spidey and Monsters Inc,
And most of the Disney characters I think.
Whenever we see him he brings us all joy.
My grandson Harry's such a cute little boy.

Love Granddad

My Dog Gizmo

I had a dog called Gizmo,
A tiny little thing.
When I came home each evening,
My slippers he would bring.

I got him through the rescue home,
He'd been mistreated, that's for sure.
But I loved him from the moment,
That he met me at the door.

He would lie there by the fireside,
With those sad appealing eyes.
Now I no longer have him,
It's only now I realise!

Just how much I miss him,
And how lonely it can be.
With no one there beside me,
Now, to keep me company.

I lost him in the winter,
When the snow was on the ground.
The vet had to destroy him,
Which was very hard I found?

I still have his basket,
And a couple of his leads.
Though I try hard to forget him,
It seems my heart still bleeds.

The Speech

Forty years Mum and Dad had been married,
Their Ruby wedding anniversary was today,
And that afternoon Mum had just told me,
A few words she wants me to say.

With a few hours left till the party,
I found it quite hard to recall.
But by pulling some words out of thin air,
I wrote a speech in no time at all.

I started welcoming all those invited,
Then I went on to praise Mum and Dad.
On the job they'd done raising six children,
Through all of those times good and bad.

With both of them nearing retirement,
And having to worry no more.
My sister got killed in a car crash,
So they brought up her family of four.

At the party, Dad jumped the broomstick,
We all laughed and cheered him with pride.
A picture was taken for posterity,
Family and friends by their side.

Panting While I'm Painting

The sweat is dripping from my brow,
As I paint the bedroom wall.
The strength is draining from me,
And I think I'm going to fall.

This summer's been fantastic,
We've not had one of late.
As I drink a pint of water,
Trying not to dehydrate.

Just standing still I'm sweating,
Phew, this weather is so hot.
I've been working since this morning,
But I haven't done a lot.

Ah, the air has gotten cooler,
I look out and discover why.
I see the sun is disappearing,
As dark clouds form in the sky.

Now it's got much darker,
Someone's turned off the lamp.
I run to get my washing in,
Before it gets too damp.

Since eight o' clock this morning,
I've been as busy as a bee.
So now it's time to take a break,
Some biscuits and a tea.

Saucy Text

Last week whilst using my mobile,
I suddenly received a strange text,
From busty Brenda from Bradford,
To myself I thought, whatever next.

Now I'm not a person of modesty,
Frigid, unworldly or a prude,
To send text like that to a stranger,
I thought was being quite rude.

So anyway I went off to Bradford,
My mate helped, he lent me some wheels.
But when I got there, I found busty Brenda,
Had trouble walking in her high heels.

I gave her a tenner for a couple of bevies,
But she didn't bring me back any change,
And whilst I was talking to Brenda,
Something else about her was strange.

Although the room was hot and humid,
All the time she was wearing a scarf.
And as we were sat there together,
People around us were starting to laugh.

When we got back to her apartment,
Which wasn't a part of the plan?
I had to scarper, quick sharpish,
It appears busty Brenda was a man.

The Lodger

I've taken in a lodger,
They say his name is Jack!
But manners in so many things,
My lodger seems to lack.

He doesn't use a knife and fork,
Whenever he eats his food,
Never a please or thank you,
In fact he's very rude.

He never seems to take a bath,
His breath it sometimes stinks,
He lies around the house all day,
He only eats or drinks.

And when it comes to sleeping,
He'll curl up on the floor.
Or any place that he can find,
But at least he doesn't snore.

Last night as he lay on the couch,
He asked me to stroke his head!
Then this morning, when I awoke,
I found him on my bed. (The cheek)

I then found him by the fireside,
He was sleeping like a log!
But to Jack these things are normal,
For my lodger is a dog.

My Achievements

Monday I climbed Mount Everest!
Ok, I climbed a hill,
But when you're sixty and Arthritic,
That's an achievement still.

Wednesday I ran a marathon!
Ok, I walked a mile.
But when I reached the shops in town,
To my face it brought a smile.

Friday I flew an Aeroplane!
Ok, it was a kite,
But the smile I got from my Grandson,
Was an absolute delight.

Today I won the lottery!
No, No, I really did!
So tonight I'll dine, on fish and chips,
As I only won six quid.

When you use your imagination,
So many things you can achieve.
All you need is lots of hope,
And a reason to believe.

My A to Z Journey Home

As I was walking home one night,
Bright lights lit up my way.
Cars were passing closely by,
Dark shadows were cast astray.
Every car that passed me by,
Formed shadows on the road.
Great giants were chasing after me, as,
Heavier became my load.

It was getting so much colder now,
Jack Frost was creeping in
Kilometres I still had to walk,
Legs now were giving in.
My way was getting darker now,
No more light, just fog and gloom.
Once over the hill, the lights of home,
Praise god I reach it soon.

Quickly I am walking now,
Rain starts falling from the sky.
Suddenly I reach my home,
Taking off my things I sigh.
Up jumps my dog and kisses me,
Very loyal to me is KING,
Waiting for me so patiently,
Xtra rations for him I bring.

Young is my heart, my body not,
Zero soon grows the hour.
As I slowly make my way to bed,
Before I lose all power.

The Guest List

With both of us reaching our sixties, a party the kids want to throw.
Both of us coming from big families, we're not sure on how many will go.
So many uncles and aunties, nephews, nieces, well you get the gist,
The missus in her infinite wisdom said she wanted to draw up a list.
With family scattered worldwide, Australia, Spain, Oh and France,
To get them to come all together, I don't think she stands any chance.
After two weeks the missus had finished, she'd given it her heart and her soul.
And with over three hundred people, it was as long as an Andrex toilet roll.
There was a person on it called Jesus, brothers Mathew, Mark, Luke and John.
Uncle Popeye and his wife Aunty Olive? The list just went on and on.
"Who's William and Katie? Elizabeth and her husband Phil?"
"Is it that rich lot from London? Will they leave us owt in their will?"
"We can't have that many people" this list was simply immense,
We'd have to hire the town hall; no way can we afford that expense.
So last night whilst the missus was sleeping, I sat down and held an inquest.
Crossing names off the said list, the missus, well, she was not impressed.
I got the list down to one fifty, a manageable amount, don't you think.
Especially as now they've just told me, I have to buy them all the first drink.
So now the missus is phoning, every family member and friend.
She never seems to stop talking, will her yakking ever come to an end?
"That was my cousin Margaret; you know the one married to Jim,"
"They live by the tower in Blackpool", "No I don't have a clue about him!"
"They're bringing Uncle Eric from Morecombe", I think that's a little unwise,
Last time he bought his new girlfriend, now there was a sight for sore eyes.
Big Hair, big bust, big mouth, it was fine till she opened her gob,
Then Auntie Elsie hit her with a handbag and fighting broke out in a mob.
Police were called to the venue; some were arrested and thrown in a cell,
We ended up paying for the damage, as the manager played merry hell.
We all spent the night in a hotel; some woke up with an incredible sore head.
Uncle Bill had more than a headache, he found the woman from next door in his bed.
His wife Susan, she went mental, he ended up in hospital for a week.
The last I heard of our Susan, a divorce she was planning to seek.

Is It Me, Or Is It My Age?

After climbing the stairs,
And reaching the top,
After pausing for breath,
And having to stop.
As it's no longer clear,
As to why you are here.
Is it me, or is it my age?

Policemen look younger,
And don't seem as smart.
You have to sit down more,
Because of your heart.
And the kids of today,
Speak in a strange way.
Is it me, or is it my age?

Whilst reading the papers,
Propped up in your bed.
You keep losing your specs,
On the top of your head.
Then somebody checking,
To make sure you're not dead.
Is it me, or is it my age.

GLOUCESTER LIFE

These are poems about the everyday things I see in and around the city as I go about my daily life. Either on my way to or from my home.

Gloucester Gaol

Gloucester have just closed their jail,
Now they've put it up for sale.
Open you can take a look,
Hurry, cause you'll have to book.
The public form a queue with pride,
To take a sneaky peak inside.

I've heard, I don't know if it's right,
Of ghoulish goings on at night.
Screaming and ringing of bells,
Ghosts in corridors and cells,
Of men who lived in days of yore,
Robber's murders and more.

They say the waiting list is long,
I'm sorry, but I could be wrong. Is this for real?
I have my doubt, fighting to get IN, not OUT.
What is this country coming to?
Excuse me while I join the queue.

(The jail will probably become a hotel like some others)

Those Digger Men

Those digger men, have started work,
Their making lots of holes,
Creating many mounds of earth,
Just like those pesky moles.

Whether it's a 360 Mac,
A Caterpillar, or JCB,
There's several models you can see,
But their all diggers to me.

Just one man and his machine,
Propelled along on tracks.
Hydraulic powered chisel tools,
For making holes and cracks.

Buckets armed with jagged teeth,
Scoop up the broken soil.
Loads into Lorries one by one,
Who take away the spoil.

They work away, tirelessly,
Manoeuvring now and then,
Doing in a single day,
The work of many men.

Jamie loves to watch them,
So we lift him up to see.
Maybe in several years to come,
A digger man he'll be.

Market Forces

They're closing our indoor market,
They say that it just doesn't pay.
But when you talk to all of the traders,
Most of them want it to stay.

The council wants to simply just close it,
And build a new TK Max there instead.
But although the traders keep complaining,
Their words go over the councillors' head.

They want to bring it to the East gate precinct,
To the 1st floor atop of the stairs,
In rooms that are standing there empty,
Where traders can still sell their wares.

The council say that current market forces,
And all the new government restraints. They've no choice but to sell off the market,
And ignore all the traders' complaints.

It's true that it does need a facelift,
In order for it still to succeed.
So many cheap shops on the High street,
A market for sure we still need.

With so many large stores all closing,
Empty shops are becoming blight,
So I say to all of the market traders,
Don't give up, keep fighting the fight.

Putting the Clock Back

They're putting the clock back over Bakers;
Its beauty is now beyond belief.
With a new coat of black Rustoleum,
And a dusting of shiny Gold Leaf.

They've cleaned off all of the figures,
And fixed the hammer held by John Bull.
And the rope attached to the large bell,
On the hour Old Father Time will pull.

They've cleaned up all of the workings,
And gave it a general spruce.
Now there's years before its retirement,
Unlike like that geezer Sir Bruce.

Let's hope that it keeps on working,
For at least another century.
That clock, that depicts all four nations,
For all of its public to see.

The Promotion

Hedley's were doing a promo,
They were giving out Coffee and Cake.
In order for the public to sample,
Their wares in which to partake.

They had so many tasters,
Sandwiches, Panini's, the lot.
And were asking the publics' opinion,
On whether they liked them or not.

I had Chocolate, Coffee and Walnut,
I went back again and again.
They'd pulled out one of the big guns,
Theo, off The Dragons' Den.

They were also asking the people,
To suggest a fair and reasonable price.
All I know from what I had tasted,
Was that ALL of their goodies were nice.

You'll find Hedley's in Gloucester,
At sixty six Westgate street,
And from all of the samples I tasted,
Their wares will be quite hard to beat.

Lady of the Seas

This beautiful lady looked so supreme,
Both on cinema and our TV screen.
Treasure Island, Three Musketeers,
She's lasted for over sixty years.
In dry dock now she's had a rest,
Now after months she looks her best.
With sails upon her tall masts three,
She's off to sail the seven seas.

The Kaskalot, built in 1948 by J Ring-Anderson for the Royal Greenland
Trading Company. She was in dry dock undergoing refurbishment by
Neilson's ship yard.

The Golden Egg

They've taken down The Golden Egg,
That blighted our Kings' Square.
Left derelict for so many years,
As if it wasn't there.

Crumbling and quite dangerous,
The thing looked a disgrace.
I wonder what the planners have,
To put there, in its place.

Some people want a toilet block,
To me, not a bad thing.
As long as it improves the place,
And new visitors will bring.

I hope, whatever they build there now,
They do so, NOW, post haste.
But consider it quite carefully,
And our money they don't waste.

The planners and the councillors,
And all the powers that be.
Whatever they decide to build,
We'll just have to wait and see.

The Doughnut

The GCHQ
Of importance is most.
It's the Central headquarters,
New listening post.
The most startling thing,
About it I've found,
There's another three storeys,
Built under the ground.

Government secrets,
Are gained and unfurled.
As they gather information,
From all over the world.
And another thing that,
I don't understand,
They read every book,
Printed in every land.

I've not seen inside it,
Don't believe that I could.
Some people have tried,
Don't think that I should.
I knew someone who worked there,
As a government spy?
If I knew what they did there,
I'm afraid I might die.

Cold-Blooded Murder

A girl was murdered last night,
In the centre of the town.
Her ex-boyfriend had stalked her,
And finally hunted her down.
People had tried to help her,
But the crime they could not stop.
As he just walked in and stabbed her,
As she worked inside the shop.

She didn't put up much a fight,
She never got the chance,
After stabbing her, he left her,
Without a second glance.
The police caught him this morning,
With the blade still in his hand,
How someone can do such a thing,
I will never understand.

The police have put a tent up,
And taped off the scene of crime.
They were interviewing people,
Who may have passed by at that time.

The camera men and TV crews,
Were like vultures at their prey,
I was watching a young police woman,
Trying to keep the hordes at bay.
A lady brought some flowers,
And left them near the scene.
With a note saying "How wonderful,
The young girl once had been".

(Hollie Gazzard was a young 20yr old local hairdresser. Since her murder the
Hollie Gazzard Trust website has been launched to raise money for GDASS,
Increase the Peace and to put 6 students a year through college.)

The Last Stagecoach from Ross

Gloucester to Hereford to Gloucester,
A round trip via the Forest of Dean.
On top of a double Decker, front seats,
So we can look at the magnificent scene.

We're doing it now for the last time,
As the number 24 route will be ending,
We were hoping that it would not happen,
But it's pointless in us just pretending.

We were waiting for the last time at the bus stop,
We were boarding the last bus from Ross.
As tomorrow they take off the service,
For the locals this will be a sad loss.

Through the villages and valley's we travelled,
Stopping off now and then on the way.
As the sunshine was lighting the scenery,
We were in for a beautiful day.

They're cutting the service tomorrow,
As they say it is no longer viable,
But the locals who work! What will they do?
Stagecoach themselves should be liable!

This can't be the only route they're running,
That is probably making a loss.
There are others that they make a profit,
Bring back our 24 route from Ross.

The Lantern Parade

Children were queuing,
With lights they had made.
All ready to march,
In a Lantern Parade.

People dressed up warm,
In hats, gloves, and tights,
All patiently waiting,
For the switch on of lights.

Streets full of people,
In rows, five, six abreast.
When the parade came in sight,
They were really impressed.

Off to the cathedral,
They amassed in the square.
What a wonderful sight,
To see them all there.

The Oxbode

There's a cow that's stuck
At the end of the lane.
With his head in the pathway,
And his feet in the drain.
The street is so narrow
The ox was so wide
They couldn't release him
But how hard they tried.

A butcher was called for
To cut up the beast
Into hundreds of pieces
"Oh what a feast."
The butcher who sliced him,
He started a sale,
And sold him as brisket,
Steak sirloin and tail.

Then up spoke the farmer
And said "Never again
Will I drive my cattle
Down Oxbode Lane."

Based on a local nursery rhyme The Oxbode was pronounced Oxbody.

FAMOUS PEOPLE

A few poems about some well-known local and world famous people.

This is a piece of art by TRIX, a local street artist. I wrote the following poem after seeing this in the street.

Nelson Mandela

Mr Nelson Mandela!
What a wonderful fella,
Lived for nigh-on one hundred years.
He did so much for peace,
And now with his decease,
South Africa mourns with its tears.

Captured by white men,
And then thrown in a pen!
For twenty-seven years of his life.
Still fighting for peace,
He gained his release!
To join up with Winnie his wife.

They called him a fool,
But he got to rule!
As soon as the Blacks got their vote.
No more Black against White!
No more reason to fight,
They should put his face on a note.

In another hundred years,
When the world's shed its tears,
Let's hope, they remember, those who can.
His long fight against Apartheid!
And they celebrate with pride,
Mr Nelson Mandela the man.

Tommy Cooper

This funny man, with deadpan face.
There's no one else who could replace,
Tommy Cooper filled us with cheer,
Attempting to make things disappear.

In penguin suit, and red Fez hat,
With a zuuh, zuuh, zuuh, and Just like that.
Upon the stage, he showed his class.
With his, Glass, Bottle, Bottle, Glass.

With those big eyes and pointed chin,
His Ha, Ha, laugh and silly grin.
It seems the whole world became fond,
Of this silly man with magic wand.

Looking like an utter berk,
With magic tricks that didn't work.
Whose antics brought grown men to tears,
Let's hope these memories last for years.

Richard III Duke of Gloucester

Richard the third, Duke of Gloucester,
For a long time now has been dead.
But they've recently dug up his body,
And now reconstructed his head.

He was found in a car park in Leicester,
At the foot of a painted letter R.
Using the latest surveying equipment,
An outstanding achievement by far.

We came face to face in the museum,
I'd never been in there before.
He was only going to be here for ten days
So I went to see him, whilst on tour.

They used computer scanning technology,
From his bones they took his DNA.
When I saw him there, looking back at me,
My mind was simply just blown away.

He's on his way back to Leicester,
Where, he's soon to lie there in state.
If you have the chance, go and see him,
I did, the experience was great.

ST Kyneburgh

Nobody seems to know her name, but long ago to here she came.
They say she was a princess royal, for whom a baker began to toil.
Her parents said marry she must, the princess thought this was unjust.
She packed her bags and ran away, and came to Gloucestershire to stay.
She looked for somewhere she could stop, and came upon a Bakers' shop,
The kindly girl they gave a home, and soon they made the girl their own.
But the baker's wife so jealous got, and very soon hatched up a plot,

Whilst the baker was away, the girl, the baker's wife did slay.
Returning home the baker found, of their young girl, no sight or sound.
He called her name to his surprise, His daughter's voice from well did rise.
Her body in the well was found, and buried in some holy ground.
The water from this well they feel, had the ability to heal.
So St Kyneburgh the girl became, on doing so she found her fame.
This monument stands here because, a miracle this surely was.
Anglo Saxon Kyne (child) burgh (royal) became Kimbrose, hence Kimbrose
Way where this sculpture stands.

Isambard Kingdom Brunel

I K Brunel was this gentleman's name,
Civil Engineering's what brought him his fame.
Though with worldwide renown, he was really quite small,
So he wore a large chain and hat very tall.

The people all scoffed, but Brunel, he knew,
That the things that he dreamed of, would soon all come true.
The Great Western Railway, his pride and his joy,
He dreamt of its building whilst still only a boy.

From Bristol to London in less than four hours,
Pulled by an engine, with steam driven powers.
The great Box Tunnel almost two miles in length,
Dug out by navvies with incredible strength.

"You'll Never Do It," the people all cried,
It cost him so dearly, one hundred men died.
On hearing what happened, to their rescue he flew,
But another collapse, almost killed Brunel too.

SS Great Britain, first propelled iron ship,
"It just won't work," the cynics all quip.
Clifton Bridge spans the Severn so wide,
Suspended from towers on rocks either side.

The first ever bridge constructed this way.
The bridge is still standing, and there it will stay,
These bridges today over rivers can span,
Because Mr Brunel was a brilliant man.

Bishop Hooper

They charged him with heresy, decided his plight,
They brought him to Gloucester to stay overnight.
Ten thousand people had come to the square,
And gathered to see what was happening there.
They placed him on pyre and told him to stand,
And secured him to stake with a big metal band.

The fire it was lit, the flames they soon grew,
His feet they got hot, and his hands soon did too.
His body did burn from his foot to his shoulder,
The wind it did blow, so the fire it did smoulder.
The fate of the bishop was all now in doubt,
As the wind it got up and the fire, it went out.

A posse was gathered, they collected more wood,
And piled it around him, at the place where he stood.
"More Fire," said the bishop, the crowd cried "ENCORE" The fire was
ignited, and it started to roar.
He pounded his chest and he started to cough,
And pounded some more till his arm it fell off.

But the bishop was strong he still was not done,
As he carried on pounding with the other one
FORTY-FIVE minutes, the bishop he fried,
At which time he gave up, and eventually died
The bishop has gone now, but never forgot,
As now we remember him, right here on this spot.

The monument can be found just outside the Cathedral entrance.

Robert Raikes

In olden days it was the rule,
Children never went to school.
In factories to work were put,
Climbing chimneys, sweeping soot.

Sundays the streets were full of boys,
Playing games and making noise.
This Robert Raikes had tried to stop,
Whilst sat above his printers shop.

The working class, weren't very bright,
None of them could read or write.
Robert Raikes being no fool,
Started up "The Ragged School".

He took the urchins off the street,
Found them somewhere safe to meet.
Some people said this was absurd,
He used his paper to spread the word.

Within two years the schools had grown,
He could no longer cope alone.
Two Bishops came to lend a hand,
And schools sprang up throughout the land.

Robert Raikes 1735 -1811
Founder of The Sunday School 1784
Buried at St Marys' De Crypt
The two Bishops were from Chester and Salisbury

The Scrooge Banker

Jemmy Wood once Haberdasher, became owner of his own bank.
Founded in Gloucester 1716, he had his Grandfather to thank.
He did business astride his shop counter, on which he had nailed down a fake coin.
As a warning to all of his customers, that his money they should not try to purloin.

He didn't like wasting his money, on fine clothes or mindless frippery,
He was known to the locals of Gloucester, as mean, tough and quite slippery.
He hitched rides for free on farm wagons, and picked up lumps of coal on his way,
He was attacked for picking some turnips, from a tenant farmers' field one day.

When new customers made a deposit, an interest rate he would deprive.
But by the end of the 1820 bank crisis, his was the only bank to survive.
He once became sheriff of Gloucester, and vowed to leave the city a large sum,
But on his death his will was contested, so that nothing of that would become.

He was named by Dickens in a novel, the one called "Our Mutual Friend",
They say it was him he based Scrooge on, who we know came to a most tragic end.
It was said he worth up to a million, He was rich, of that there's no doubt,
But was often mistaken as a vagabond, whenever he was out and about.

He will go down in the history of Gloucester, as a man who is known by a few,
But if you mention Scrooge the Banker, everyone knows him, surely that's true!
He was mean, ruthless, but wealthy, seen as an entrepreneur even back then,
Like the ones you see today on the TV, on that programme, *The Dragons Den*.

A spitting image puppet of Jemmy Wood can be found in St Michael's tower on Gloucester cross.

Willie Wonka

His name was Willie Wonka, he owned a factory,
That made the finest Chocolate bars, and strange confectionary.
He held a competition, children from Countries near and far,
Searched to find a Golden Ticket, wrapped around a Wonka Bar.
They thought that they had found them, it seems that was a lie,
It appears that one of them was fake, so they had another try.

A young boy called Charlie Bucket, who lived with his old Gramp,
In a broken down ramshackle house, which was so cold and damp,
Bought a lucky Wonka bar, with the last penny that he had,
Given him for his birthday, from his loving old Granddad.
The owners of the tickets were taken on a tour,
Of Willie Wonka's Factory, where such wondrous things they saw.

Little men called oompa loompa's, were working vast machines,
Producing lots of tasty treats, you find in childhood dreams.
Rivers flowed with Chocolate, they walked a candy laden street,
It seemed that everything they saw, was possible to eat.
Although they didn't know it, the four were on a quest,
The others failed along the way, but Charlie passed the test.

Now Charlie and his Granddad, knowing that they had won,
Were told by Willie Wonka, that their journeys just began.
They took a glass elevator, which reached into the sky,
Breaking through the glass domed roof, they found that it could fly.
Charlie and his grandfather, could not believe their eyes,
Then absolutely dumbstruck, finding Wonka's factory was the prize.

Guy Fawkes

On November the 5th in Britain we try,
To remember an event, by burning a Guy.
Fireworks are lit, in the darkness of night,
Bursting like flowers with colours so bright.
Rockets explode high up the sky,
But does anyone today, know the real reason why?
In London the politicians were greedy and fat,
It was decided to kill them, right there, where they sat. Guy Fawkes and his
men came up with a plot,
Whilst parliament sat, they would blow up the lot.
They broke into tunnels that went under the street,
Placed barrels of powder, right under their feet.
Thirty Six barrels were placed in a row,
And primed with the fuses, already to blow.
But Guy did not know there would soon be a hitch,
As one of the gang, it seems, was a snitch.
The alarm was raised, and Guardsmen were brought
He tried to escape, but Guy, he was caught.
He was hung by the neck until he was dead,
But not only that, they cut off his head.
Before end of day and the rise of the moon,
His stomach was sliced and his guts were all strewn.
They still were not happy, so, just to be sure,
The rest of his body was cut into four.

This is known as hung, drawn and quartered; a very gruesome way to die.

Father Christmas

When Father Christmas comes to town,
With long white beard and bright red gown.
Trimmed with Ermine, purest white,
He must truly be a wondrous sight.

With reindeer pulling sleigh of toys,
To give to all GOOD girls and boys.
With magic dust to help them fly,
So speedily across the sky.

As midnight strikes, through homes he'll creep,
Whilst all GOOD children are asleep,
Filling sacks, and stockings hung,
Till finely his work is done.

You must never open eyes to see,
Or very cross Santa will be!
If during night sleigh bells you hear,
For Santa will not come next year.

WORLD EVENTS

These are poems about some of the tragic things that have happened over the last century. Most thought provoking I hope.

This picture is taken from the war memorial at Gloucester Cathedral.

Those Soldiers Brave

They fought in battles those men so brave,
Whose names are mentioned on this grave.
So that for us our lives could keep,
On beaches and in trenches deep.

Up to their knees in freezing mud,
Amongst dead and dying all covered in blood.
Those friends they had made or already knew,
Ordinary people just like me and you.

From every city, small village and town,
Whilst the bombs, and bullets, just kept raining down. Those soldiers brave,
both young and old,
In the heat of the desert, and winters so cold,

Whilst nurses and doctors to the wounded did tend,
They just kept on fighting, right up to the end.
So remember the men whose lives they gave,
Those men young and old, Those Soldiers So Brave.

The Great War

One hundred years ago, saw the start of a war,
That of which the world had not witnessed before.
Millions of men to the front lines were sent,
To fight against an enemy, who it seems, were hell bent,
On causing mayhem, and destruction where ever they went.

Dug into trenches, eight feet or more high,
With nothing to see, except only the sky.
Soaked to the skin, with cold rotting feet,
Only tea to drink, and Bully Beef to eat
Chocolate and Cigarettes, were their only treat.

All around them, the injured left dying in blood,
Whilst the cannons and horses got stuck in the mud.
Over the trenches, the bullets and shells pass,
But thousands of men, each day, suffered alas,
As into their lungs they breathed Mustard Gas.

As the men fought in trenches, so cold and dank,
They heard the sound of this thing, called a tank,
Which no one had seen, but would soon get to know.
As it stood there before them, their fears start to grow
They're unable to run, as there's nowhere to go.

As it trundles towards them, the ground starts to shake,
Leaving rubble and destruction behind in its wake.
Glued to the spot, they start to tremble with fear,
As the massive machine, draws more and more near,
And their fate on that day, became evermore clear.

Angels of the Battlefields

Young girls still only in their teens
Dressed in pristine white.
Working non-stop for many hours,
Throughout the day and night.

In wards of field hospitals,
That were no more than just a tent.
Saving the lives of soldiers,
From the battle they'd been sent.

Surgeons in the theatres,
With hardly any tools,
Often working without sleep,
And ignoring all the rules.

Many men had injuries,
They had not seen before,
Some of them, blown to bits,
Oh the atrocities of war.

All working in conditions,
They'd had no time to rehearse.
Caring for the injured,
The voluntary nurse.

Over the Top

We stood in the trenches all waiting,
For the endless shelling to relent.
And at six, when the signal was given,
Over the top, we were all sent.

In a minute our dead were ten thousand,
They were all piling up in a heap,
The German soldiers had been hiding,
In concrete bunkers so deep.

The first lot were cut down in seconds,
Mown down in the heavy German fire.
Others were ripped to shreds, struggling,
Tangled up the razor sharp wire.

As we struggled towards German front lines,
Crawling through the mud and the dead.
My mate Tommy, who was there, close beside me,
Was killed by a shot to the head.

I took one in the shoulder,
So I waited some minutes to see.
If anyone came to my rescue,
Or what fate had in store for me!

So many men that day were slaughtered,
Twenty thousand, they say, maybe more.
Sacrificed by the Brigadiers and Generals,
Grown men who were playing at war.

Abandon Shipping

ABANDON all shipping,
The country is slipping,
Eight hundred more people on dole.
Is anyone listening?
No point in resisting!
The plug has been pulled from the hole.

For heavens' sake!
Sir Frances Drake,
Would be turning now, in his grave.
It was hell of a shock,
To the large Portsmouth Dock,
But now it's too late to save.

They put in a plea,
To the now BAE,
In the hope of a second chance.
But no one is listening,
No point in resisting,
They are all in their villas in France.

May day, May d ay, May day

He was now all alone in the aircraft,
And the airport was looming ahead,
They'd only gone off on a day trip,
Now the pilot beside him was dead.

Mayday, Mayday, Mayday!
The call went out to the tower,
They needed someone to guide him,
So he flew around for an hour.

They sent him over to Humberside,
Where they had everything he would need,
With all the emergency services,
They could land him there they agreed.

An RAF helicopter was watching,
And showed him which way he should go,
But just how all this would be ending,
As to yet, no one there was to know.

A pilot instructor talked to him,
And told him how he could steer,
But John Wildely was now seventy-seven,
Whether he'd make it was their biggest fear.

After his first failure at landing,
He tried it again and again,
Then finally on the fourth time of trying,
He managed to bring down the plane.

The Winter Olympics

Every day, for the next two weeks, you can see on your TV,
From Russia, the Olympic Games, which is coming from Sochi.

First there's Alpine Skiing, also called the Downhill Race.
Where they negotiate through gates, at such fantastic pace.

Then we have Cross Country, and the Biathlon.
Where shooting at a target, medals are lost or won.

And then we have Ski Jumping, where men and women try,
After leaping off a giant ramp, see how far they can fly.

Next we have the Free style, on the Moguls and the slopes,
Performing tricks high in the air, on which they pin their hopes.

Then there's Figure Skating, the men and girls look nice,
As together and then singularly, test their skills upon the ice.

Next we have the Hockey, where two teams will chase a puck,
Zooming around at breakneck speed, and score a goal
with luck.

There's also the Speed Skating, on short or long speed tracks,
Trying to finish first, across the line, and not upon their backs.

We also have the Sliders, Bobsleigh, Skeleton and Luge,
Hurtling down the icy slopes, around walls of ice so huge.

Last we have the Curling, played with strategy and skill,
They throw the stone, then sweep the ice, to guide it where they will.

Each one of them is different, in skills of some degree,
So I sit back and admire them, as an athlete I'll never be.

The Clutha

It dropped like a stone,
But no one knows why!
The Police helicopter,
Was unable to fly.

Crashing through the roof,
Of the full Clutha pub,
As hundreds of people,
Were enjoying their grub.

Ten people were killed,
And lots more were hurt,
It could have been worse though,
And that's a dead cert.

Police, Ambulance, and Firemen,
Were quick on the scene!
With survivors and helpers,
They worked as a team.

Pulling out the people,
And sitting them down!
Midst the chaos and mayhem,
Of this large Glasgow town.

So many families,
With loved ones so dear!
Will be left broken hearted,
What with Christmas so near.

Philippines Disaster

I was watching TV,
Whilst eating my tea.
And I saw all those people in trouble.
Those poor Philippines,
With no method or means,
Help needs to be sent on the double.

It made their hearts wrench,
From the sight and the stench,
Of litter and bodies all strewn.
With no water to drink,
I was starting to think,
Help better get to them soon.

They spoke to this man,
Hit by Typhoon Haiyan.
Robbing him of children and wife.
What's left now for him?
Where does he begin?
Just how do you start a new life?

Ukrainian Crisis

The state of the Ukraine is in crisis,
As yesterday on the news we all saw,
The Red Army has gone into the Crimea,
Looks like that they're heading for war.

Russian troops have surrounded all barracks,
Stirring up, even more violence and hate.
Whilst an army of tanks line up waiting,
Ukrainian troops were just stood at the gate.

Why Putin has sent his troops in there?
Well myself, I just dread to think.
With the Ruble sinking evermore faster,
His economy teeters now on the brink.

With Putin and his cronies in the Kremlin,
Making their decisions of late,
The European countries are all gathering,
To kick Russia out of the G8.

Let's all hope that nothing comes of it,
And everything ends up with peace!
That man learns to live with each other,
And the warring and fighting will cease.

Man's Inhumanity

No one could imagine,
What role it would play,
As high over Japan, flew the Enola Gay.
Carrying its cargo,
Like a pregnant mother.
As the world was to see,
What we could do to each other.

Four hundred children,
In one school got surprised,
As the H bomb was dropped,
They were all vaporised.
Nothing was left of them,
Not even their clothes.
As the blinding light hit them,
And the mushroom cloud rose.

No lessons were learnt though,
You'll still see today,
As political leaders,
Their war games still play.
Can somebody tell me?
Just what is God's plan?
Why must we still suffer?
Man's inhumanity to man.

Enola Gay was a World War Two, B29 bomber which dropped atomic bombs on both Hiroshima and Nagasaki. The bombs were dropped at 8.30 am at a height that would cause the maximum damage to humans and property. The plane was named after the pilot's mother.

Flight MH 370

It took off at zero hour twenty,
The pilots set the course it should steer,
As it left from Kuala Lumpa airport,
The weather ahead of them was clear.

They say it flew for over an hour,
No one knows what happened it seems,
As Malaysian flight MH three seventy,
Disappeared off all radar screens.

How the hell can a plane of that size?
Simply disappear out of all sight.
A voice from the cockpit was recorded,
As a pilot said "All right Good night."

It looks like they might have found wreckage,
But, why exactly did it go where it went?
Was it down to a mechanical failure?
Or a terrorist with intensions hell bent!

After three weeks of frantically searching,
By airplanes and ships, of the seas,
And satellites scanning the areas,
There is no news of survivors to please.

It's like looking for a needle in a haystack,
There're things that we still need to know,
Was it an accident, or intentional?
What did happen to flight MH 370?

Crown of Thorns

They made him carry his own cross,
With crown of thorns on head.
Then crucified him on the hill,
And left him there till dead.

As he hung upon the cross,
Between the other two.
He said "Father please forgive them,
For they know not what they do."

They took him down by six o'clock,
That was the Sabbath day.
Placing him inside a tomb,
With large stone in doorway.

On Sunday, Mary Magdalene,
Walked stealthily through the street,
With water and clean bandages,
To wash his hands and feet.

When arriving at the tomb,
The large stone was not there.
Reaching where he'd lain inside,
She found the tomb was bare.

Now Mary Magdalene was scared,
Of capture, and of prison,
A voice said "Be ye not afraid,
For Jesus Christ has risen."

They Travelled Far

To Bethlehem the couple came,
His wife upon a mule;
They had to sign a register,
At that time this was the rule.

They travelled more than seven days,
Then finally reached the City;
They found it hard to find a room,
No one would give them pity.

They eventually found a kindly man,
Who owned a local inn.
He gave them room inside a barn,
Where, her labour did begin.

She gave birth to a baby boy,
In the middle of the night.
Above their heads, there rose a star,
The brightest ever light.

The animals all gathered round,
And went down on their knees.
They knew the baby was to be king,
And now him they tried to please.

Three kings arrived, each bearing gifts,
From far off they had rode.
Each one bowing down to him
With, Myrrh, Frankincense, and Gold.

On December 25th this year,
Whilst kids with toys all play.
Tell them what it's all about,
Remember Christ's Birthday.

THAT'S LIFE

A few poems all about the things that happen in our everyday lives. Some are fact, some are fiction. They are all based on things I have encountered during my time on this earth.

Victorian Life

In Victorian Times,
The living was hard.
In a two up, two down,
With a tiny backyard.

Children were working,
Sixteen hours in the mill.
And still had to work,
Even when feeling ill.

Climbing through machinery,
In dangerous conditions.
Loosing fingers or limbs,
With the help of Physicians.

Young girls, young as twelve,
Were put on the street.
And sold to old men,
Like pieces of meat.

Whilst the gentry were feeding,
On roast pheasant and wine,
The working class people,
Were still towing the line.

People caught stealing,
A small crumb of bread,
Were sent to the prison,
Or the Americas instead.

The Burlesque Show

On Sunday afternoon I went,
To see inside Der Spiegeltent.
A Burlesque Cabaret was on,
So took my place with some aplomb.

A table to myself, not bad,
So lots of room and food I had.
We started off with bubbly drinks,
This is looking good (me thinks).

The acts come on and start cutting a dash,
Singing and dancing with poise and panache.
Then I realise that it's all been a ploy,
It's all been a trick, it's a girl not a boy.

The waitress comes with sandwiches thin,
So many there are, where do I begin?
The crowds sounding happy and looking quite pleased,
There's singing and dancing, a little striptease.

Here's the waitress again with cakes on a tray,
Boy this is fun I think I shall stay.
The last act is on "WOW what a girl"
With hips that gyrate and tassels that twirl,

The crowds going wild and calling for more,
It's really quite saucy and not even four.
It's all over now so off I must go,
But overall, a really wonderful show.

The Petrol Head

My nephew Nick is a petrol head,
There's nowt more he would like.
Than sitting in a motor car,
Or sat astride a bike.

He doesn't really mind at all,
As long as it's got power.
Going round a racing track,
At two hundred miles an hour.

He likes to hear their engines roar,
And give out lots of noise.
There's nothing he likes better than,
Being out there with the boys.

He takes new owners, and their bikes,
And puts them through their paces.
The one thing he enjoys the most?
The smiles upon their faces.

The Game

On most Saturdays,
All over the land.
Thousands of people,
Will sit down or stand,
For almost two hours
Watching men chase a ball,
Football or Rugby,
It's simply their call.

Travel hundreds of miles,
Following their team.
Whoever they support
They all have one dream.
Gaining promotion and going up,
Winning a trophy, the league or the cup.

But if their team is beaten,
No doubt you will find,
The linesman was biased, the referee blind.
Whatever they're watching,
It's always the same,
Calm down you people,
It's only a game

Aunty Pat's Cat

Now my Aunty Pat
Has got a large cat.
It's coat is rather quite bushy.
At night when at home,
When she's all alone,
She really likes stroking her pussy.

Now her boyfriend Tim!
Who's really quite dim,
Calls it his little fur ball.
Thinks it only polite!
To feed it two times a night.
And Pat doesn't mind that at all.

Now my Aunty Pat's cat,
Is getting quite fat!
Was it something in the food that it loves?
Now her boyfriend Tim!
Said "Don't blame it on him"
He didn't know he should have worn gloves.

Cheltenham Literature Festival

Friday I arrive in T shirt of lime green,
I'm a volunteer now and part of the scene.
Our task is to set up and ready the tent,
Before curtain up of the first main event.

On Saturday I'm sent to the front of the queue,
And usher the people to doors one or two.
The people go in and start taking a seat,
The tension gets higher and so does the heat.

Sunday is here I'll go in early (me thinks),
Ray Davies is on (frontman of The Kinks).
Then when that's over it's off I will go,
To Alexander and Richard from that Pointless show.
Next Emma Thompson and I'm taking a look,
And get her to sign as I've just bought her book.

Monday evening and I'm wasting an hour,
There's a talk on the Ashes it's by David Gower.
I meet Johnny Vegas the man off TV,
The one with the monkey, who's flogging the tea.
Tuesday I get busy and roll up my sleeves,
And give myself blisters from raking up leaves
Ok finished now so I'm off for a walk,
To Doug Allan and his wildlife photography talk.

Wednesday Andrew Marr the political bloke,
He's drawing and painting after having a stroke.
Whilst walking, I meet up with wildlife's Kate Humble,
Ask for her autograph and try not to mumble.
I'm off now till Sunday, I'm taking a rest,
I'm so blummin' tired, it's probably best.

Sunday is here, Robert Winston I'll see,
He's talking about Science throughout History.
Now off to the Relish for breakfast to take,
Bacon bap, coffee and small piece of cake (£8.00)
The afternoon's here, now where do I go?
AAH, that amazing Burlesque Cabaret Show.
It's going quite well, they're aiming to please,
There's singing, acrobatics a little striptease.
The last act is on now, WOW what a girl,
With hips that gyrate and tassels that twirl.
The crowds going wild their begging for more,
It's really quite saucy for twenty to four
Now it's back to work and what's next for me?
Jennifer Saunders and Derek Jacobi.

It's all over now, but no time to play
We're all busy tidying and putting away.
The party has started there's plenty of beer,
Goodbye everybody I'll see you next year.

Can I Trust My MP?

Can I trust my MP?
I would like to think I can!
Although I wouldn't buy a car off one,
Be they a woman or a man.

You see them on the TV,
When they talk in many tongues.
Telling us to "Trust in them",
Whilst susceptible to bungs.

They tell us "We must all face cuts",
Then, before our very eyes,
Using magicians' sleight of hand,
Give themselves a big pay rise.

Living in two houses,
With their wives on the payroll.
They fiddle their expenses,
Whilst *we* sign on the dole.

They live the life of Riley,
Attend banquets, drink fine wine,
Back home, to feed his wife and kids,
A man resorts to crime.

They say they will do this, and that,
But once they've got our vote,
They lose their manifesto,
On the paper it was wrote.

The Open Door

Most days of the week,
Between twelve and two.
I meet up with friends,
And we pull up a pew.

There are a few places.
Where we like to meet,
To get a hot drink,
And a quick bite to eat.

A coffee or tea,
A soup and a roll.
Because life can be hard,
When you're stuck on the dole.

The Salvation Army's,
A good place to go.
With kind hearted people,
That you'll soon get to know.

There's the Park St Mission,
Brunswick Baptist Church.
You'll find many places,
If you care to search.

So if your cold, or lonely,
Or you just need a feed.
There's a door always open,
If you're ever in need.

Hate Mail

I went on line the other day,
To check up on my mate,
All I saw on her web page,
Were messages of hate.

Calling her all sorts of names,
And other hateful lies.
Reading all this bullying,
I can't believe my eyes.

Not only was there verbal abuse;
They've put pictures on there too.
Now she's shut inside her room,
Not knowing what to do.

Now she thinks of suicide,
By not reporting it to staff;
Her so-called friends still bully her,
And think it's all a laugh.

On Guard

Everyday he'll sit there,
Outside his masters house,
Keeping a close watch out,
For any bird or mouse.

He doesn't ask for payment,
Just food and a warm bed.
And just in case it's raining,
Access to garage or the shed.

When they come back from going out,
He'll give a gentle purr.
Then rub himself against their legs,
And cover them in fur.

Like those guards outside the Palace,
In thick fur coat as well as hat.
He'll guard the house from dawn till dusk,
For he's their friendly loving cat.

The Panto

In Britain, every Christmas time,
We have this thing called pantomime,
With custard pies and the usual jokes,
Men dressed as women, and women as blokes.
There's always a villain, whom the kids, boo and hiss,
The prince or the princess, who always get their kiss.

Somewhere in the production, it amazes me how!
They manage to include, a goose, horse or cow.
But the star of the show is always the Dame,
Whatever the panto, it's always the same.
Then there's the lead boy, who's played by a girl,
All this cross dressing, just makes my hair curl.

First Cinderella, who's the down trodden lass,
After attending the ball, leaves a slipper of glass,
With pumpkin for a carriage, and mouse for a horse,
And two ugly sisters, shush, "they're men of course."

Then there's Aladdin, young thief come tramp,
Who comes into a fortune, after finding a lamp.
Meets up with a princess, and goes for a ride,
On his magic carpet, then takes her for his bride.

Next there's the panto, sometimes called Puss In Boots,
All about young Dick Whittington, who had Gloucester roots.
Both him and his cat, travelled to London, WHERE!
The young boy did good, and soon became Mayor.

Whatever the panto, they're always good fun,
With plenty of laughter, for your daughter or son.
You'll hear plenty of clapping, cheering and boos,
So go out and see one, you've got nothing to lose.

Flights of Fancy

(The Red Bull Flugtag)

They come from every point on Earth,
And launch themselves, for what it's worth,
From end of pier, into the sea,
And a giant bird pretend to be.

With wings of cardboard,
Strapped to their arm.
They gather speed,
With some alarm.

Some with faces,
Racked with fear!
Only to plummet,
Off end of the pier.

With woops of derision,
Or cheers of delight!
Some are successful,
And actually take flight.

Flugtag is German for Flight Day. It is an annual event held in several countries. The idea is for a team to launch their handmade human powered machines off a pier into the water.

The world record for flight is 258ft.

The Bamboo Tree

In Japan a gardener went to work,
He toiled each day, and did not shirk.
And then one day, with smile on face,
Put a Bamboo plant, in pride of place.

For years he fed and nurtured it,
Under its shade would often sit.
And as the gentle breeze blew each day,
The Bamboo tree would dance and sway.

One day the gardener, said to the tree,
"I've something sad to say to thee,"
He stroked the tree, then said with frown,
"The time has come to cut you down."

"OH NO, OH NO," cried the Bamboo tree,
PLEASE, DO NOT do such a thing to me?"
The gardener said, "Please understand,
I need your help to till the land!"

"For years I've fed and watched you grow,
Now I've other seeds I need to sew."
The Bamboo tree then bowed his head,
And to the gardener, he gently said.

"For all your love, my thanks to you,
Now go do, what you have to do."
He cut it down with just one swipe,
And from it, he made a water pipe.

The gardener built a chute by hand,
To help irrigate his fertile land,
For months and months he did not stop,
And from his seed, he grew his crop.

Fight the Good Fight

Fight the good fight, with all your might,
That's what some people say.
Just shrug aside the little things,
That life puts in your way.

Each hurdle put in front of you,
Just take it in your stride.
And when somebody blocks your path,
Just push them to one side.

And as you get much wiser,
As life goes on each day!
You'll learn to use the little tricks,
You pick up along the way.

Refuse to let them get you down,
No matter how they try.
And if at first you don't succeed,
Still hold your head up high.

Wear your heart upon your sleeve,
And keep it there with pride.
Then, even if you lose the fight!
At least you'll know you've tried.

The Horrid Scene

As we were walking out one day,
We came upon a horrid scene,
A young child had walked into the road,
And had hit a cars windscreen.

It seems he tried to cross the road,
Along with his young mate.
He hadn't stopped to look each way,
And so befell his fate.

The ambulance and police had come,
And closed off all the road.
The witnesses just stood there shocked,
As he lay there, icy cold.

They rushed him to the hospital,
Where, doctors and nurses tried,
Their very best to save his life,
But alas the young boy died.

Next time your child is playing out,
Without the use of chaperone.
Make sure that they can cross the road,
And the highway code their shown.

A Prayer

Oh Lord, when I ask of you,
Why don't you answer my prayer?
Now I wonder at times,
If you're really up there.

So I ask of you Lord,
From your soul please divest,
Is this punishment for all?
Or just some kind of test?

So much war and destruction,
On this planet the Earth.
Are you telling us, This is,
What your son's life is worth?

How can I repay you?
What more can I do?
I've given you my soul!
Now the rest's up to you.

I ask nothing grand Lord,
Just the basics of life.
That you protect my family,
My home, my children, my wife.